MARVIN HAMLISCH
Songbook

GLENVIEW PUBLIC LIBRARY

3 1170 00316 1290

D1470316

ISBN 0-7935-1061-9

784.5
HAM

Hal Leonard Publishing Corporation

7777 West Bluemound Road P.O. Box 13819 Milwaukee, WI 53213

© 1992 by HAL LEONARD PUBLISHING CORPORATION
International Copyright Secured   All Rights Reserved

For all works contained herein:
Unauthorized copying, arranging, adapting recording or public performance is an infringement of copyright.
Infringers are liable under the law.

Glenview Public Library
1930 Glenview Road
Glenview, Illinois

APR 1 9 1993

photo by Martha Swope

A Chorus Line

"Best Picture of the Year"

They're Playing Our Song

WINNER OF 7 ACADEMY AWARDS

E STING

Featuring the Music of

COTT JOPLIN

Music Conducted & Adapted by
MARVIN HAMLISCH

The Way We Were

Contents

y Thompson

BIOGRAPHY

In the 1960s it was "Sunshine, Lollipops and Rainbows," the hit song recorded by" Lesley Gore, and other pop singles, as well as the beginning of a career scoring motion pictures, with The Swimmer.

In the 1970s it was the theme song and score for the motion picture The Way We Were (which earned two Academy Awards), and his musical adaptation of Scott Joplin's music for the film The Sting (which earned a third Academy Award).

Later in the decade came A Chorus Line, which won the composer the Tony Award, the New York Drama Critic's Circle Award, the Theatre World Award and the Pulitzer Prize, and is the longest-running Broadway show in history.

Still in the 1970s came his second Broadway musical Neil Simon's They're Playing Our Song.

In the 1980s were film scores and musical adaptations for Ordinary People, Sophie's Choice (nominated for an Academy Award) and Three Men and a Baby.

And now the 1990s will reflect more and different talents, dimensions and visions of Marvin Hamlisch.

"Music can make a difference," Hamlisch says. "There is a global nature to music which has the potential to bring all people together. Music is truly an international language, and I hope to contribute by widening communication as much as I can." One Song, a 'global' anthem,' with lyrics by Alan and Marilyn Bergman, was written as an anthem for all people.

Marvin Frederick Hamlisch was born on June 2, 1944, in New York City. He and his sister, Terry, were raised in a musical household by their father, Max, an accordionist and conductor, and their mother, Lilly. In this musical setting, Marvin began playing the piano at the age of five. He began lessons at age six and was admitted to the Juillard School of Music at age seven — one of the youngest students ever to be admitted to that school.

His piano lessons continued for fourteen years, after which he embarked upon a B.A. in music composition at Queens College, where he graduated *cum laude* in 1967. During those teenage years, he happily discovered that it was composing songs which inspired him. One of his earliest inspirations, a pop single, came out around that time; entitled "Sunshine, Lollipops and Rainbows," it was sung by Lesley Gore and held a solid position for more than eleven weeks in Billboard's Top 100 chart for 1965.

In 1968, while playing the piano at a party being given by film producer Sam Spiegel, Hamlisch discovered that Spiegel was in search of a composer for his new Burt Lancaster film, The Swimmer. Three days later Hamlisch presented Spiegel with his music theme for the motion picture. Spiegel hired Hamlisch on the spot, and suddenly the young composer was in Hollywood, writing the tunes instead of playing them.

> *"Music can make a difference...it is truly an international language, and I hope to contribute by widening communication as much as I can."*

Marvin Hamlisch's first years in Hollywood were marked by a prolific output which included music composition and/or adaptation for such films as Take the Money and Run, Bananas, Save the Tiger, The April Fools, and Kotch. The latter film featured the song "Life Is What You Make It," written with Johnny Mercer, which earned Hamlisch his first Academy Award nomination, as well as a Golden Globe Award.

On the evening of April 2, 1974, during the live television broadcast of the Academy Awards, audiences around the world were given their first introduction to Marvin Hamlisch when he came up to the podium to accept his first Oscar... and then his second... and then his third. It was on his last trip up to the podium that Hamlisch leaned into the microphone and quipped, "I think we can now talk to each other as friends."

Two of the Oscars he received that evening were for his work on The Way We Were, directed by Sydney Pollack and starring Robert Redford and Barbra Streisand. In addition to providing the film's score, Hamlisch collaborated with the husband-and-wife lyric-writing team of Marilyn and Alan Bergman to create the movie's memorable title song. Barbra Streisand's recording of "The Way We Were" went on to become her first million-selling single.

Hamlisch received his third Oscar that evening for The Sting, George Roy Hill's con-man caper starring Robert Redford and Paul Newman. For The Sting, Hamlisch evoked the perfect blend of nostalgia and fun by adapting the music of ragtime's master composer, Scott Joplin. The widespread success of The Sting soundtrack album (featuring "The Entertainer" as its theme) provided the country with a re-introduction to the magic of ragtime, as well as renewed appreciation for the works of a neglected

American composer, Scott Joplin.

Hamlisch's success at the 1974 Oscars was repeated at the Grammies that year, where he received four Grammy Awards including: Best Song of the Year ("The Way We Were"); Best New Artist; Best Pop Instrumental ("The Entertailler"); and Best Original Score (The Way We Were).

In 1975 Marvin Hamlisch decided to return home to New York, to take a shot at Broadway. His first shot was A Chorus Line.

As conceived by director/choreographer Michael Bennett, A Chorus Line celebrated in terms s both stark and glorious the unsung heroes and heroines of Broadway — the chorus line of dancers without whom no Broadway musical could fly. Their real-life stories, drawn from hours of marathon rap sessions conducted by Bennett, became the basis upon which Bennett, Hamlisch, co-authors James Kirkwood and Nicholas Dante, and lyricist Edward Kleban built their musical.

Opening at the Shubert Theatre on Broadway on July 25, 1975 after a spring tryout at Joseph Papp's Public Theater, A Chorus Line became an overnight sensation, receiving unanimous raves from the critics, showered with accolades and tributes, and adored by ecstatic theatregoers. For his contributions to A Chorus Line Marvin Hamlisch received the Tony Award, the New York Drama Critics' Circle Award, the Theater World Award and the Pulitzer Prize.

In September of 1983 A Chorus Line became the longest-running show in Broadway history. In December of 1985, with the show still going strong in its eleventh year on Broadway, the motion picture version was released. During those years, the music of A Chorus Line moved beyond Broadway and into the popular arena; a Broadway ballad, "What I Did" For Love," had become a pop ballad, while a Broadway anthem, "One," became a national anthem for TV variety shows, pops concerts and school pep rallies everywhere.

Marvin Hamlisch followed his very big Broadway debut with an intimate musical comedy which featured only two characters. He was an Oscar-winning composer; she was a talented lyricist. In true "art imitates life" fashion, this musical's comical romance took it's cue from the true-life romantic entanglements of Oscar-winning composer Marvin Hamlisch and his talented lyricist, Carole Bayer Sager.

The team of Hamlisch and Sager were joined by Neil Simon, as the musical's author, and with Robert Klein and Lucie Arnaz in the starring roles, They're Playing Our Song opened at the Imperial Theatre on February 11, 1979, and very quickly became everyone's song. They're Playing Our Song flourished on Broadway (where it ran for over 1000 performances), in London, in national tours criss-crossing the country for several years, and in hundreds of stock and regional productions since.

Hamlisch has composed film scores and/or adaptations for more than 30 films, including Woody Allen's Take the Money And Run and Bananas, Save the Tiger, Kotch, The April Fools, The Spy Who Loved Me (including the film's hit single, "Nobody Does It Better," recorded by Carly Simon), and Ice Castles.

His television credits have included the signature theme for ABC's breakfast time news program, Good Morning America, and scores for the NBC adaptation of Osborne's The Entertainer starring Jack Lemmon, and the ABC adaptation of Tennessee Williams' Streetcar Named Desire starring Ann-Margaret and Treat Williams.

Marvin and his wife Terre reside in New York City.

THE WAY WE WERE

(From The Columbia Pictures, Rastar Production "THE WAY WE WERE")

Words by ALAN and MARILYN BERGMAN
Music by MARVIN HAMLISCH

Copyright © 1973 by COLGEMS-EMI MUSIC INC.
All Rights Reserved

WHAT I DID FOR LOVE

(From "A CHORUS LINE")

Mucis by MARVIN HAMLISCH
Lyric by EDWARD KLEBAN

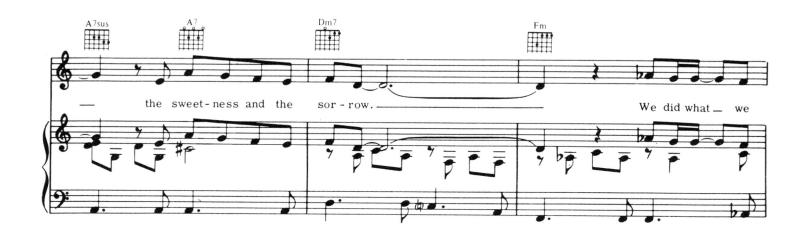

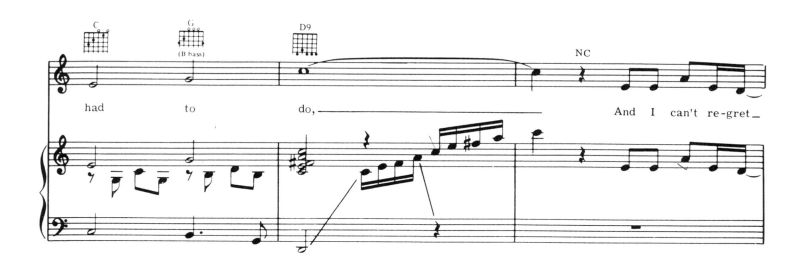

© 1975 MARVIN HAMLISCH, INC. and EDWARD KLEBAN
All Rights Controlled by WREN MUSIC COMPANY and AMERICAN COMPASS MUSIC CORP.
International Copyright Secured   All Rights Reserved

ONE
(From "A CHORUS LINE")

Mucis by MARVIN HAMLISCH
Lyric by EDWARD KLEBAN

© 1975 MARVIN HAMLISCH and EDWARD KLEBAN
All Rights Controlled by WREN MUSIC COMPANY and AMERICAN COMPASS MUSIC CORP.
International Copyright Secured   All Rights Reserved

SWEET ALIBIS

Words by CAROLE BAYER SAGER
Music by MARVIN HAMLISCH

Copyright © 1977 by Chappell & Co., Inc., Red Bullet Music, Unichappell Music and Begonia Melodies Inc.
This arrangement Copyright © 1991 by Chappell & Co., Inc., Red Bullet Music, Unichappell Music and Begonia Melodies, Inc.
All Rights Administered by Chappell & Co., Inc. and Unichappell Music, Inc.
International Copyright Secured   All Rights Reserved
Unauthorized copying, arranging, adapting, recording or public performance is an infringement of copyright.
Infringers are liable under the law.

(From the Columbia Picture "ICE CASTLES")
THEME FROM

ICE CASTLES
(Through The Eyes Of Love)

Words by CAROLE BAYER SAGER
Music by MARVIN HAMLISCH

Copyright © 1978 by Gold Horizon Music Corp. & Golden Torch Music Corp.
International Copyright Secured   All Rights Reserved

THE ENTERTAINER
(From The Movie "THE STING")

Music by SCOTT JOPLIN
Arranged and adapted by GUNTHER SCHULLER
As recorded by MARVIN HAMLISCH

Copyright © 1974 by Deshon Music, Inc.
Used with Permission   All Rights Reserved

NOBODY DOES IT BETTER

(From The Movie "THE SPY WHO LOVED ME")

Lyrics by CARLY SIMON
Music by MARVIN HAMLISCH

Copyright © 1977 DANJAQ S.A.
All Rights Controlled and Administered by EMI U CATALOG INC. and EMI UNART CATALOG INC.
International Copyright Secured   All Rights Reserved

IF YOU REALLY KNEW ME

Words by CAROLE BAYER SAGER
Music by MARVIN HAMLISCH

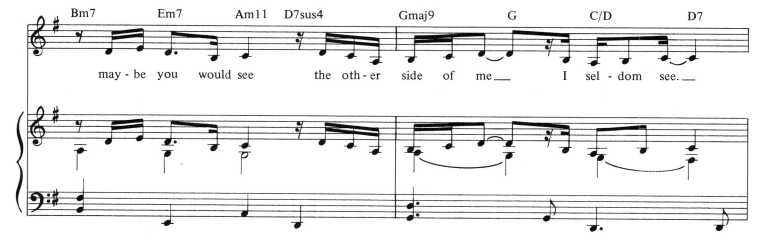

* Female singers may substitute "he" wherever "you" appears.
   Male singers may substitute "she" wherever "you" appears.

Copyright © 1979 by Chappell & Co., Red Bullet Music, Unichappell Music, Inc. and Begonia Melodies, Inc.
Red Bullet Music administered by Chappell & Co.
Begonia Melodies, Inc. administered by Unichappell Music Inc. throughout the world.
International Copyright Secured   All Rights Reserved
Unauthorized copying, arranging, adapting, recording or public performance is an infringement of copyright.
Infringers are liable under the law.

If you real-ly knew__ me, if you'd take the time__ to un-der-stand, may-be you could find me, the part I left be-hind me, may be you'd re-mind me of who I am.

FALLIN'
(From The Musical "THEY'RE PLAYING OUR SONG")

Lyric by
CAROLE BAYER SAGER

Words by CAROLE BAYER SAGER
Music by MARVIN HAMLISCH

I'm a-fraid to fly, and I don't know why, I'm
think by now I'd learn, play with fire you get burned,

jeal-ous of the peo-ple who are not a-fraid to die. It's
fire can be, oh so warm, that's why I re-turn.

Copyright © 1979 by Chappell & Co., Red Bullet Music, Unichappell Music, Inc. and Begonia Melodies, Inc.
Publication and allied rights administered by Chappell & Co., and Unichappell Music, Inc. throughout the world.
International Copyright Secured   All Rights Reserved
Unauthorized copying, arranging, adapting, recording or public performance is an infringement of copyright.
Infringers are liable under the law.

THE LAST TIME I FELT LIKE THIS

(From "SAME TIME, NEXT YEAR")

Words by ALAN BERGMAN and MARILYN BERGMAN
Music by MARVIN HAMLISCH

Copyright © 1978 & 1979 by Leeds Music Corp.
Print rights throughout the world controlled by Chappell & Co.
International Copyright Secured   All Rights Reserved
Unauthorized copying, arranging, adapting, recording or public performance is an infringement of copyright.
Infringers are liable under the law.

IF YOU REMEMBER ME

Words by CAROLE BAYER SAGER
Music by MARVIN HAMLISCH

Copyright © 1979 by Chappell & Co., Red Bullet Music, Unichappell Music, Inc. and Begonia Melodies, Inc.
Publication and allied rights administered by Chappell & Co. and Unichappell Music, Inc. throughout the World
International Copyright Secured   All Rights Reserved
Unauthorized copying, arranging, adapting, recording or public performance is an infringement of copyright.
Infringers are liable under the law.

SUNSHINE, LOLLIPOPS AND RAINBOWS

Lyric by
HOWARD LIEBLING

Words by HOWARD LIEBLING
Music by MARVIN HAMLISCH

Copyright © 1963 by Charles Hansen Educational Music & Books
(A division of Charles Hansen Music & Books, Inc., New York, NY)
All rights for the world, excluding U.S.A. and Canada, controlled by Campbell, Connelly & Co. Ltd., London, England
International Copyright Secured   All Rights Reserved

THEY'RE PLAYING MY SONG

(From "THEY'RE PLAYING OUR SONG")

Lyric by
CAROLE BAYER SAGER

Words by CAROLE BAYER SAGER
Music by MARVIN HAMLISCH

Copyright © 1979, 1980 by Chappell & Co., Inc., Red Bullet Music, Unichappell Music, Inc. & Begonia Melodies, Inc.
Publication and allied rights Administered by Chappell & Co., Inc. and Unichappell Music, Inc. throughout the World.
International Copyright Secured
Unauthorized copying, arranging, adapting, recording or public performance is an infringement of copyright.
Infringers are liable under the law.

THE MUSIC OF BEING FREE
(FREEDOM IS)

By ALAN and MARILYN BERGMAN
and MARVIN HAMLISCH

Copyright © 1990 Red Bullet Music and Threesome Music
All Rights for Red Bullet Music controlled by PolyGram International Publishing, Inc. (3500 West Olive Avenue, Suite 200, Burbank, CA 91505)
International Copyright Secured   All Rights Reserved   Made in U.S.A.

ONE SONG

By ALAN BERGMAN,
MARILYN BERGMAN and MARVIN HAMLISCH

Copyright © 1990 Red Bullet Music and Threesome Music
All Rights for Red Bullet Music controlled by PolyGram International Publishing, Inc. (3500 West Olive Avenue, Suite 200, Burbank, CA 91505)
International Copyright Secured   All Rights Reserved   Made in U.S.A.

DREAMERS

Words by CHRISTOPHER ADLER
Music by MARVIN HAMLISCH

Copyright © 1983 by Steamy Night and Red Bullet Music
Administered by Chappell & Co.
International Copyright Secured   All Rights Reserved
Unauthorized copying, arranging, adapting, recording or public performance is an infringement of copyright.
Infringers are liable under the law.

Glenview Public Library
1930 Glenview Road
Glenview, Illinois